YAHYA TEACHES KHALID ABOUT SABR

YAHYA TEACHES KHALID ABOUT SABR

Umm Yahya

Copyright © 2025 by Umm Yahya

All rights reserved. No part of this book may be reproduced in any manner whatsoever without written permission except in the case of brief quotations embodied in critical articles and reviews.

First Printing, 2025

This story has been written by Umm Yahya and edited by Maya Hughes.

The illustrations have been created by Umm Yahya with the help of Ces Rosanna Price.

This book is dedicated to my father Habibur Rahman Torofdar, who is an ongoing example and inspiration for me as someone who displays the beautiful characteristics of sabr. He is known to many as being very quiet and patient, especially during difficult times—the hardest being when he lost his companion of 52 years, my late mother. He is still dealing with her loss and, alongside this, other health problems, but still displays a beautiful patience.

May Allah (SWT) reunite everyone with their loved ones in Jannah and ease everyone's suffering and hardships. Please keep my father in your duas. May Allah (SWT) give us all the ability to face challenges with sabr and reward us immensely for our efforts. Ameen.

بسم الله الرحمن الرحيم

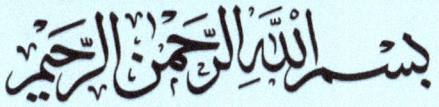

It was a perfect weekend for a family treat and Yahya and Khalid had been waiting eagerly for the annual Summer Funfair event. They loved the cheesy chips, stalls and most of all, the funfair rides of course!

Before getting into the car, they remembered to bring their pocket money they had earned in the last few months. They had saved it all to spend at the funfair because Mum always said that she was happy for them to buy toys with money they obtained for their hard work.

Strapping up their seatbelts, they looked ahead to see the satnav, which said that the funfair was only 20 minutes away.

"Ahhh yes! The funfair isn't far. What do you want to do first, Yahya Bhaiya?" Khalid screeched with excitement.

"Shall we go on the fire truck ride that you love? The one where you can ring the bell?" Yahya suggested.

"Oh, I love that one. I hope the funfair has it," wished Khalid.

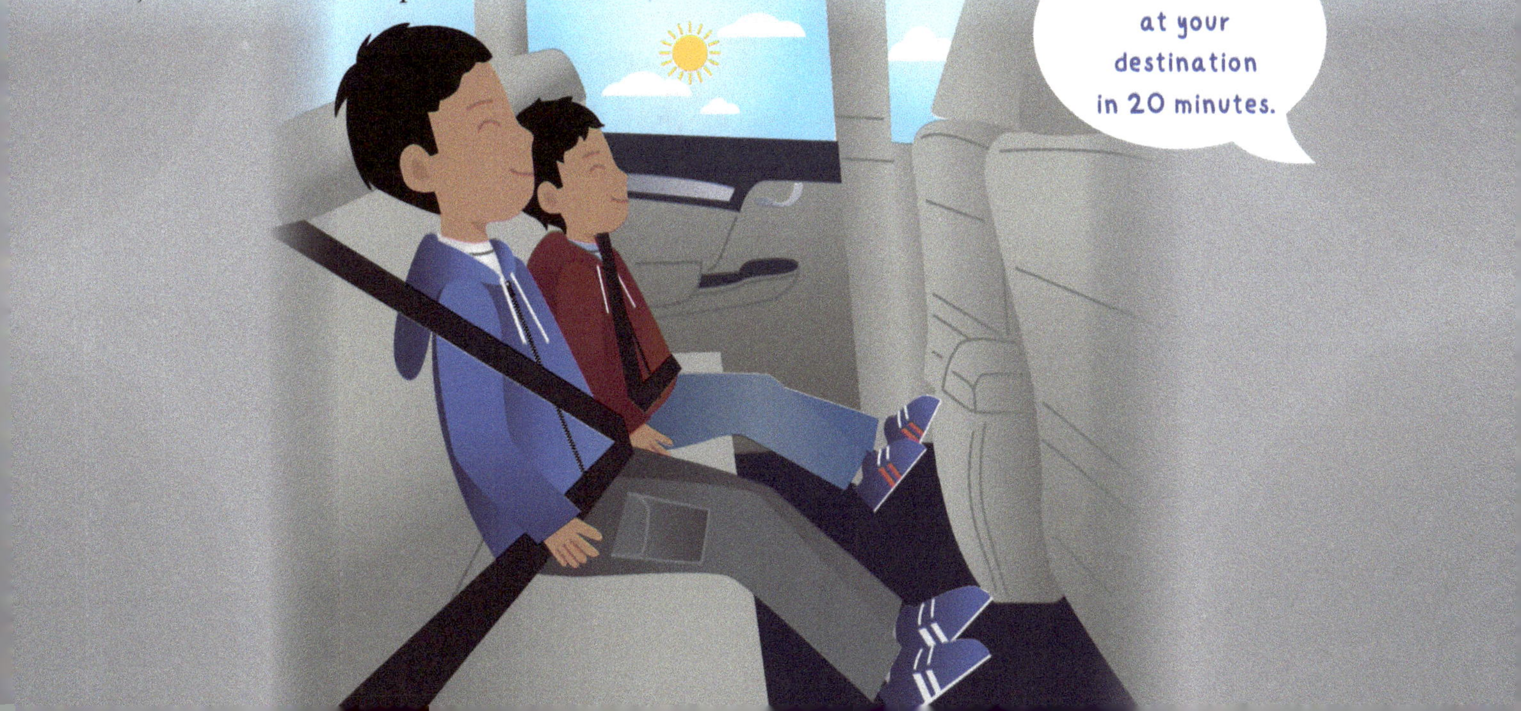

After around five minutes, the short journey they were hoping for suddenly seemed less likely. There was loud machinery on the road because of roadworks and all you could see were orange vehicles, signs and cones. The steadily flowing traffic came to a stop and the road was filled with buzzing car horns.

"Ohhh noooo… We're stuck in traffic and now it says we have 35 minutes left! We're never going to get there," grumbled Khalid.

"Don't worry, Khalid. I know you really want to go to the funfair, and I do too, but we just need to have sabr and, In Sha Allah, we will be there soon," explained a calm Yahya.

"Sabre? Sabre-toothed tiger? We need to roar at the traffic?" enquired a slightly confused Khalid.

Yahya started chuckling, but he stopped himself because he didn't want to upset his brother, and so he continued.

"No Khalid, not the tiger. Sabr. Sabr is when we have patience and don't get angry or upset at what's happening. Like now, when we're stuck in this horrible traffic."

"But we're going to be late and everyone will go on the rides before us!" replied Khalid, who was still upset.

"I know you love the rides but the funfair is open all day, so please don't be disheartened. Did you know that in the Quran, in Surah Al Imran, Allah (SWT) says, 'And Allah loves the patient.' So, Khalid, we should always try to be patient in hard times, even if it's not our fault, because Allah (SWT) loves this and He will reward us," explained a wise Yahya.

"Like now," he continued. "We're stuck in traffic—not because of us, but probably because lots of other people want to go to the funfair too. So we have to be patient with the situation."

Khalid stayed silent with a perplexed look on his face, not really knowing what to do next. The traffic wasn't moving and there wasn't anything to do in the car to make time go faster.

Mum and Dad suggested playing some games to make the time pass more quickly. The boys loved the idea, so they played I spy and a game where they had 20 questions to guess an object.

Khalid started with: "I spy, with my little eye, something beginning with 'B'…"

The boys started getting competitive, forgetting all about the traffic and not realising that they were, in fact, practising their patience.

After they had passed two road workers drilling, the traffic slowly cleared and the lines of cones became smaller and more distant.

They finally arrived at the funfair and, to no one's surprise, there was a long queue at the entrance. As Dad was paying for the parking, Mum and Yahya strolled up to join it, while Khalid was dragging along behind, letting out little disappointed sighs.

"Khalid, don't be disappointed," his brother consoled him. "Remember what I told you in the car about sabr. I also want to teach you another line from the Quran. In Surah Az Zumar, Allah (SWT) says 'the patient will be given their reward without measure,'" Yahya explained with such calmness and belief that their day was going to get better.

"Ok, Bhaiya. I'm going to be a sabr!" promised Khalid.

"Oh Khalid, you're so funny! You can't *be a* sabr; you have to *have* sabr!" Yahya replied, while gently and lovingly holding his brother's hand as they walked closer to the entrance.

Finally the moment had come. They were just about to cross the entrance when a funfair marshal stopped them. Khalid let out a huge groan and his heart sank. He was certain that they weren't going to let any more people in. Then, to his surprise, the marshal began to apologise with some good news.

"We're so sorry you've been waiting in this queue for so long. We'd like to offer your family and everyone behind you some free ride tokens to apologise for the long wait," announced the funfair marshal.

"Wow! Thank you, thank you, thank you!" Khalid repeated, as he jumped up and down in amazement.

Yahya looked at him and smiled. Khalid stared back at his brother, pointed his finger to the sky and mouthed, "sabr," with a super proud face, knowing that the mercy of Allah (SWT) was shining down on them, and they were rewarded with something they didn't expect—free ride tokens!

As they entered, they could see that the funfair was decorated in mesmerising lights, with refreshment stands letting out appetizing whiffs of delicious, hot food. The colourful toy stalls were full of children, scurrying around, not knowing what to choose.

Khalid and Yahya ran over to the loudest section of the funfair. They went on the fire truck ride first, as Yahya had suggested earlier, followed by the carousel, spooky train, and finally the inflatable castle. They happily used their free tokens, which instantly made the day more enjoyable.

After conquering all of the rides, they ran over to buy some toys. The boys spent time sifting through the baskets full of pocket money items and finally decided to buy some miniature cars and Lego building kits.

After finishing their tokens and spending their pocket money, they felt a bit peckish, so they asked their dad if they could get some food. Striding over to the food trucks, they stood in line to get some cheesy chips and halal burgers.

Nearby, they could hear some stomping, and there, tugging at his mum's hand, stood a little boy, complaining.

"I'm hungry," he whimpered. "I don't want to wait… Why can't we just go to the front?"

You could see his mum trying to explain the rules of waiting in a queue and being fair to others.

Yahya and Khalid could hear the whole conversation and looked at each other and said one word: "sabr." The brothers giggled, and Mum smiled in the knowledge that they were now thinking the same thing.

It was getting late, so they grabbed all their goodies from the funfair, including buckets of candyfloss and popcorn, and they started walking back towards the entrance. They got into the car, all ready to go home, but the car park was jammed full of cars, all trying to leave at the same time.

By now the boys knew exactly what they had to do. They didn't moan, sigh, grumble or huff and puff. Instead, Khalid inquisitively asked his brother a question:

"What did Prophet Muhammad (SAW) say about sabr?"

Yahya responded with a smile.

"I'm so glad you asked that Khalid. Let me tell you. Prophet Muhammad (SAW) was the best example of patience. Throughout all the hard times in his life, he had sabr and continued to believe in Allah (SWT) and know that Allah (SWT) would fix his problems. There was an incident in Ta'if where people didn't like him talking about Islam or Allah (SWT) and they pelted him with rocks, twigs and rubbish, to try to hurt him and drive him out of the city of Makkah. But he didn't fight, shout or throw anything back because he knew that patience would be rewarded."

Khalid listened attentively while Yahya carried on.

"Prophet Muhammad (SAW) said, 'The best of faith is patience.' This means that the best Muslims are the ones who have sabr when life is difficult. They have sabr because they know and believe that this is Allah's (SWT) plan and that He only wants goodness for us. So sabr is not just about being patient but also about believing in Allah's plan and timing for everything," Yahya explained.

"So, do you mean that if something happens which makes us sad or angry, we should know that it will actually be good for us, because it is Allah's (SWT) plan and He knows what's right for us?" Khalid summarised maturely.

"Yes, exactly, Khalid. Ma Sha Allah—you're learning. So let me tell you one last thing before you get too tired, and because it's the most important thing," Yahya said seriously.

"Go on Bhaiya, I'm listening…" Khalid replied.

Yahya's voice lowered in respect while he uttered the Arabic words: "Fa sabrun jameel. A beautiful patience. We should be patient in difficult times, but our patience should also be beautiful. We should be content with whatever is happening, without complaining, and trust in Allah (SWT). The people of Palestine are also a perfect example of this that we should try to follow in our lives."

"Oh, I know why you say that Bhaiya. I've seen a video where, even though their houses have been broken to pieces, they are still smiling and praying to Allah (SWT) in amongst all of the rocks," Khalid quickly interrupted.

"Exactly this, Khalid. They have sabr in the most beautiful way. They could be sitting crying, non-stop, and complaining, but they have hope and continue to thank Allah (SWT) for their blessings. May Allah (SWT) reward them for their struggles. Ameen," Yahya concluded.

"Ameen," Khalid copied.

Slowly, the cars exited the car park and were all making their way home. It had been a really fun day at the funfair, but also a very educational one.

As the sky got darker and the wind rustled, the boys looked out of their windows in deep thought about their day. Yahya looked over to the left to see Khalid rubbing his eyes and letting out a yawn; he was definitely ready for bed. By now, he would normally have started getting restless in the car, but softly you could hear the words leave Khalid's mouth…

"Fa sabrun jameel."

Discussion:

1. Why did Yahya and Khalid's journey to the funfair take longer than expected?

2. Which ayah did Yahya teach Khalid from Surah Al Imran?

3. What was the good news that the marshal had for Yahya and Khalid?

4. Which ayah did Yahya teach Khalid from Surah Az Zumar?

5. What did Khalid learn about the Prophet and sabr?

6. What is the Arabic for 'a beautiful patience'?

7. Can you think of a time when you had to have sabr? What happened?

8. How will you practise patience during the next difficult time in your life?

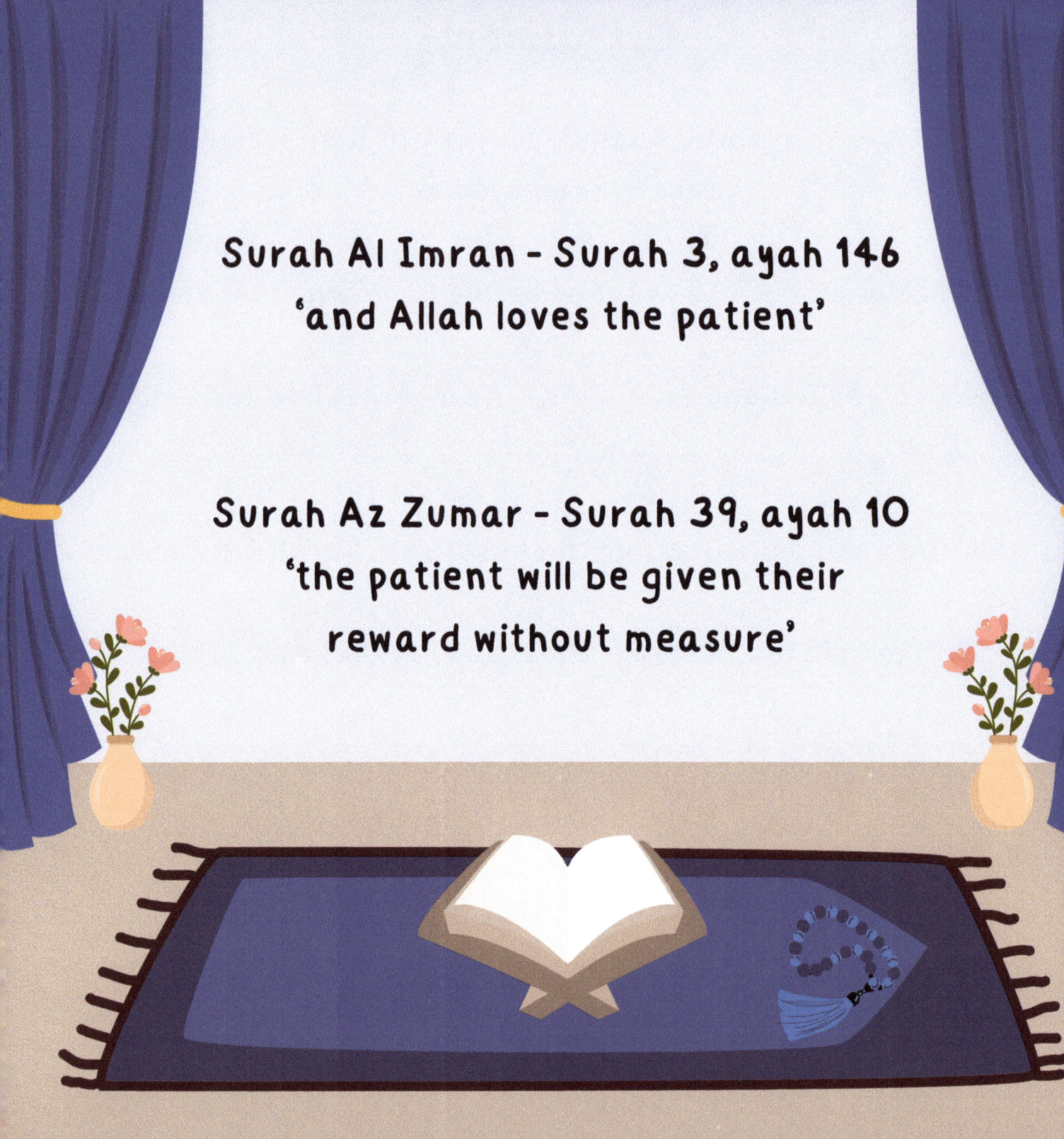

Prophet Muhammad (SAW)
'The best of faith is patience.'

FREE PALESTINE

فصبر جميل

Fa sabrun jameel
A beautiful patience

This story has been created to teach children about the characteristics of sabr (patience) from an early age. Throughout life, everyone will face many challenges, some sooner and some later than expected, but we will have to get through the hardships we are tested with. Whether we are young or old, we will need to implement sabr at many moments in our lives.

Every child will face difficulties in life, whether they are small, like waiting in traffic jams, or big, like troubles with friends, health and family. This book will hopefully teach them about a beautiful patience that they can implement in their lives from an early age, so that hardships in the future will be easier to deal with, In Sha Allah.

www.ingramcontent.com/pod-product-compliance
Lightning Source LLC
Chambersburg PA
CBHW061158010526
44119CB00059B/854